Job Interview
To-Do-List

A Simple Makeover for Anyone
Preparing for a Job Interview

By D.L Warren

ABOUT THE AUTHOR

D.L. Warren has worked well over 30 years in a technical field within a large government organization and has over 25 years' experience working in management and leadership roles. During that time she has run numerous job competitions at all levels of the organization. With Behaviour based interviewing being a predominant method of interviewing she has substantial knowledge and experience on preparing and conducting the interviews. She has a lot to offer from a "cross the table perspective" on how to prepare and succeed at a job interview.

DISCLAIMER

Why People Do Not Do Well at Job Interviews

There are many reasons why people do not do well at job interviews and I can pretty much sum it up to not doing the necessary research and preparation for the interview. Many people will walk into an interview and sink themselves within the first few minutes by what they do or do not do. In addition, most do not know the difference between a behavioral based and a situational based question and consequently do not answer them correctly. Or worse yet, leave a question unanswered which means no points if your interview is being graded. There are many do's and don'ts that may seem like common sense, but still people fall into the trap of not knowing what they are, basic information for doing well at an interview.

Another common problem is not putting together all the necessary material and knowledge that you will need to do well. It is not sufficient to have all the technical skills ready when you have made a really bad impression within the first 60 seconds of your entrance that sits in the interviewer's mind throughout the interview. That is a killer but it does happen.

In this book I will provide you with many tips including a To-Do-List approach to getting ready for your next interview. All the information I will give you is relatively straight-forward, and the key to your success will be following the steps provided and preparing for that next great job you will succeed in getting.

Time to Take Charge of Getting your Next Job

The trick to getting good results is to be as prepared as possible for your next job interview. You want to be as thorough and efficient as possible in the preparation hence the to-do-list approach.   It will take time on your part with a starting time months before the job interview.

Employers recognize the costs of training new employees as well as the cost of letting someone go, so they want to get it right the first time. This will require from them a planned approach to the hiring process. Hence you need to be prepared for an interview that has been well thought out and delivered. If you do not have the skill in one or more of the areas that will be tested it is critical that you discover this well in advance of the interview so you can go about getting the experience. It will be too late to achieve a competency at the last moment.

Once you finish the book, set a plan of action that is timely, thorough, doable and specifically targeted at your next job. Make a commitment to yourself, prepare and then follow through. I am not suggesting that it will be super easy but if you do you will reap the rewards.

About The Book: Job Interview To-Do-List

The goal of this book is pretty simple, I want to assist you in understanding what is necessary for preparing for a job interview. I will guide you through lots of information for your preparation, however the challenge will be for you to put the information to use. Do the research and make a plan that will identify all the tasks and time frames and then complete the necessary items.

By the end of this book my hope would be that you understand what is necessary to walk into an interview and feel totally comfortable at what you will be faced with. You will know the difference between answering situational or behavioural based questions and will have prepared for all the areas that you will be questioned on. In addition you will succeed at making a good impression and not sinking yourself at the get go by understanding the do's and don'ts of interviews.

The information in this book is fairly basic and easy to understand, but it will take some work on your part to prepare for the interview. The first task will be understanding what is necessary and then make it into an actionable plan. Get your to-do-list out and start jotting down some of the ideas as you work through this book.

TABLE OF CONTENTS

CHAPTER 1

PREPARING FOR AN INTERVIEW

In this chapter I cover the initial items you will need to start preparing for your upcoming interview. This could be for an interview that you have already scheduled or one that you are intending to get in the future. I will cover all the preparatory work necessary and items that you will need to do well before the interview date.

Getting Organized

The first call to action is to develop a plan of what is necessary in getting ready for the interview. I might suggest that you prepare your to-do-list, which will include an itemized listing of what will be required over the next several months. The job you may be looking for may not even be posted at this time, but you want to be prepared in the event that the interview schedule is set for only weeks following the posting. It doesn't really matter as to how you record the information, just ensure that it is easy to access and follow. Some find that keeping all information in a binder for reference works for them while others start a spreadsheet on their computer. The key is to find a way that works for you and use it regularly throughout the process.

To assist you in getting started download a sample To-Do-List checklist available at www.lynnhallbooks.com.

Goals and Schedule

List all your goals on one side of your spreadsheet and then break them down into tasks that are associated with the larger goal. You may have numerous tasks assigned to each goal. For example, if your goal is to study a particular reference guide, you may want to list your goal as Study Reference Guide, and then in the task column list each of the chapters as a particular task. There is no right or wrong way to do this it is only important that all the tasks are identified, and broken down into bite size pieces. By doing this you are able to track your progress and feel a sense of achievement.

Beside each of the tasks identify the time frame for completion. It is important to set realistic time frames. Do not make your plan overly ambitious but at the same time have target dates that meet your intended need. You may want to set up small as well as larger tasks in your plan. The key to small tasks is that you can sneak them in even when you do not seem to have a lot of time and they keep you motivated to achieving your larger plan.

Your time frames may be set up as to what suits you best. You may want to target items on an hourly bases or daily tasks or ones that target a one week time frame. Remember to put them down in writing and stick to them. It is amazing how a week can go by and without keeping yourself accountable poof the time is gone without the work being done.

Staying Motivated

*"Applying for a job can be stressful,
how can I keep myself motivated despite
endless setbacks?"*

It is important that you stay motivated through the process but critical that you do stay balanced and healthy. Keep other important activities in your life in your schedule and stay true to them. You may have family obligations that will also need to be honoured. Stay healthy, lots of sleep, eat properly and exercise will keep you on the right track of success.

One of the keys to success is ensuing a good support network. Let others in on your goals and ambitions. They can be friends, coworkers and family. Let them know how you are doing both on the positive side or if you feel any setbacks. The support network will come in handy for encouragement as well as serve as a resource perhaps for asking you sample questions and listening to your proposed by the end of this book my hope would be that you understand what is necessary to walk into an interview and feel totally comfortable at what you will be faced with. You will know the difference between answering situational or behavioural based questions and will have prepared for all the areas that you will be questioned on. In addition, you will succeed at making a good impression and not sinking yourself at the get go by understanding the do's and don'ts of interviews.

Research the Job

One of your first goals will be to fully understand the job that you are applying for and how that particular employer conducts interviews. The better you understand what the employer is looking for in a candidate the better you are in preparing for the interview.

Ask other Employees

"Can researching current employees prior to my interview work to my advantage?"

Do your research on the job, what are the qualifications they are looking for, what are the working conditions, what background knowledge and experience are typically expected for the positions and what is the culture of the organization. As an example some companies typically expect people to work beyond set quitting time to get the job done while other companies would never expect this. Everyone usually knows these norms and if your desires are to finish at 4 o'clock regardless of the job this might not go over big in a company with other norms. Essentially the culture is "how we do things around here" and it will serve you well to try and glean as much knowledge as you can before going into the interview.

Reach out to people that are in the same job or similar jobs and let them know your intensions. I believe most people are really interested in sharing information about the job they are in and helpful to others that are looking to choose that career. Ask them what type of interviews the company typically holds, what questions they pose and what you can expect from the process. Keep notes and add them to your research.

Ask the employer

Do not be afraid to contact the employer and find out how they typically conduct interviews. Although companies will vary it is typically the hiring manager or human resource manager that will be able to assist you. Ask what technical information will they be asking during the interview? Will the questions be behaviour or situational based, are there different competencies that will be covered, how can I prepare for the interview? Do not be afraid to pose the questions as the worst that happens is that they do not share. I always found that employers like to share this type of information as they want candidates to do their best as it makes the selection process that much easier. I would much prefer that a person has time to prepare an answer well in advance so that time is not wasted during an interview as they try formulate an answer on the spot. The employer is not trying to trick the candidate only gather as much pertinent and relevant information as possible so that the right person can be selected for the position.

One of the primary reasons for checking as early as possible for what the job interview will entail is so that you can prepare well in advance. For example, if there are many books that questions may be based on you need to know this so you can set up your study schedule. Another key reason is that if questions are going to be based on various skills and abilities you want to ensure that you are prepared. For example if you are required to show that you have 'initiative' do you have this in your skill bag? If not, you can start a plan of action to acquire this skill. Understand fully what the skill, or competency is then start to demonstrate this at your current job. The more time you set this into action the better you will be able to use this should this skill be tested.

From Internet and Other Sources

If you are in a position where you cannot obtain the information from an employer try searching on the internet. You will be able to find the skill and knowledge set typically required for a position. You may be extra lucky and actually find a job posting that is similar to the one you are seeking. Use the information provided to set your plan in place.

References

"Who should I be using for my references?"

Plan to select people that you know will give you a positive and if possible glowing reference either personal or work related references. Many people have not been successful at getting a job as the result of negative items that have come up on the reference check. It is key that you ask permission of your references as no one wants to be caught off guard receiving a call without the courtesy of being asked. It is a good idea to ask your reference what they would say about you. Ask them how they would respond if they were asked about your dependability, initiative, work habits etc.

Another good habit is to give your reference a copy of your resume as this will make them more prepared to answer questions, and do not forget to let them know when you are going for the interview as you may have established the permission well in advance of your interview.

In this chapter I have covered what it is to start the process of getting prepared for your interview. You should now know how to set up a to-do-list and have an idea of what goals and tasks will be listed along with the timeframes for each. You understand that you will have to know all about your proposed job and hopefully have gathered insightful information on what you can expect from the interview. The next chapter will take you a step closer to understanding the types of questions you should prepare for.

CHAPTER 2

UNDERSTANDING JOB INTERVIEW QUESTIONS

There are different types of interview questions that you many encounter during your interview. The most common will be straightforward knowledge, ability and skill questions but that might not be the end of what you should expect. In this chapter I will cover what situational based questions are and the (relatively) new kid on the block, Behavioral Based Questions (BBQ). I say they are new, but in fact they have been around for 30 odd years but frequently find their way into the interview process. It is critical that you understand these types of questions so that you are ready for any questions posed to you.

Knowledge, Ability and Skill Questions

These types of questions are straightforward and are structured to find out a bit more about you. What is your background, your skill set, test your knowledge and your technical skill set. In addition there may be questions that are designed to find out personal attributes. How well to you work in a team or get along with others or are there any work performance issues. Keep in mind that any questions you will be asked may also be assessing communication skills. I have included examples of some of the questions a bit further on in this book.

Situational Based Questions

Most people are familiar with situational based questions being asked during an interview. It is simply a hypothetical situation being asked and you provide to the best of your ability as to how you would handle or deal with the situation. Employers use these types of questions to see how well you understand a process and how you would deal with situations. The benefit of situational questions for the interviewee is that they do not really have to demonstrate that they have actually carried out the behaviour it is just necessary to know the steps and provide a convincing scenario as to how to execute the procedure, although one would hope this is how you would handle a situation. If properly prepared for the question you can simply list off the various components and this should be sufficient. For example,

- *How to mobilize your team?*

If you learn how this should be done, you can provide an excellent response even if you have never been in a situation where you have had to do this.

Behavioral Based Questions

Behavior Based Interviews were developed about 30 years ago and although they have changed somewhat they are still being used largely today to assess competencies. The premise for their popularity is that it has been shown that people typically will keep the same behaviour patterns overtime. So, the questions in the interview are all about asking you how you have handled different situations in the past. You are expected to describe a situation that actually took place. This is different than asking you how you would handle a situation where you could recite a book and get all the right points, but in reality you may never behave in that manner.

In the interview you will be asked several questions that will be used to assess your skill, ability and knowledge. The response to the question must be based on your performance from a previous situation. They are not interested in an answer that poses what you might do in the future.

Many employers are using the behavioral based questions so it is imperative that you are able to understand how they work and be ready to answer them during an interview. Employers do like this type of questions as they are getting a better understanding of who you are and how you handle various situations. In some cases you will be asked to provide a reference to a person that can verify the story that you are telling. In the early days of behaviour interviews this was always expected but many employers are not requiring them. I suspect the reason is the amount of work it takes to verify each question answered. Nevertheless, when you are preparing your answers, always have in the back of your mind the possibility of having to provide a name of someone who could verify your information.

When you are formulating your responses to a behaviour based question it is best to prepare for at least two scenarios for each question. One may be sufficient but it does not hurt to have an additional one prepared just in case the first answer did not quite fit what they were looking for and you get asked to provide an additional response. Here are a few examples of behavioral based questions.

1. *Tell me about a time when you had to use your presentation skills to influence a decision maker.*

2. *Tell me when you had to go above and beyond the call of duty to get your job completed.*

3. *Tell me about a difficult decision you had to make and implement. What was the outcome?*

4. *Give me an example of a time when you tried to accomplish a task and it failed.*

When preparing for the questions you want to make sure that you are using examples that are as current as possible. If you have recent examples that are from your current workplace those responses would be the best. The next best would be from a previous employer and that followed by an example from outside the workplace. For example, if the question is on Leadership, you may not have any examples from your current place of work particularly if you are not in a leadership role. However, you may have been a manager at your last job and this is where you could draw upon to come up with your answer. If you find that you have never been in a leadership role at work but were a coach on a soccer team, this may be a place where you could show you leadership qualities.

Role Playing

Role playing questions are set up so the interviewer can assess how you would handle various situations. For example, the interviewers may play the part of an angry customer and you must play the part of the employee. Your reaction to the situation is being assessed so carefully think how you would handle the situation. You can use the material you have prepared for your behaviour questions to assist you in how you would respond.

During your preparation for your interview if you believe that these types of questions will be asked it is very important that you practice with your friends or family. It sometimes is difficult to respond to these questions as not everyone is comfortable in this play acting. By practicing you will get the hang of it and not feel uncomfortable in the interview.

In summary you should now be familiar with the different types of questions that are likely to be asked during your interview. If this material is new to you add a task on your to-do-list to review and become familiar with the different types of questions so that it becomes second nature. You do not want to confuse a behavioral based question with a situational based question during the interview.

CHAPTER 3

INTERVIEW QUESTIONS: BASIC QUESTIONS

Basic Questions to be prepared for

Prepare and Practice Introduction.

Do not overlook this important part of the job interview as I have witnessed people sink themselves at the get go for making inappropriate comments at the beginning of the interview. It would really shock you. First impressions are made very early on and once you have made a bad impression you may not be able to recover. Humor is a really good quality however, when you are an unknown person what might be acceptable once people know you can come off quite unacceptable during an interview. I recommend that you script your introduction, but try not to have it come across as scripted when you introduce yourself. Have your support system (family, friends) take a look at it or even practice on them to get their impression. It seems like such a small item but it can be a showstopper.

Why you want the job?

Employers are looking for value added to their company. What do you have to offer? This is a question you should ponder and prepare a good response. Find out as much as you can about the company, about the industry. This will show that you are interested and committed to this company.

1. *Tell why you are interested in this line of work.*

2. *How did you become interested?*

3. *Tie in your long-term goals and your passions.*

4. *Everything else being equal to the next interviewee, what is it that would make you standout.*

What do you have to offer to the position?

Employers are looking for someone to fill a position, your job will be to convince them that person should be you. Below I will explain further on behaviour based questions that you will need to prepare for that are specific to certain skills and abilities, but in general have a list of your experiences and skill set accomplished at work and elsewhere.

Tip:

- *Keep a mental list of all your accomplishments and link them into benefiting the company's goals*

- *Link in your passions into the job requirements*

This question is likely to be assessed during the behaviour based interview questions, but it is not a bad idea to think about a response and be ready should you be faced with it directly. Even if it is not asked sometimes the ideas can be woven into the conversation that will make you stand out.

Prepare a question to ask at the Interview.

It is always a good idea to be prepared to ask a question at the end of the interview; this sends the signal that you have done your homework and are very interested in the position. Ask questions that pertain to the job such as:

1. Describe the company's leadership philosophy?

2. What is the typical career progression for a person in this position?

3. What would you say are the most important skills necessary to exceed in this position?

4. Does the company offer training?

5. How can I best contribute to the company?

If you do not have a question or two prepared it can send a bad signal to the interviewers. It might suggest that you are not interested in the company or the employee/employer relationship. To some degree it can suggest that you lack confidence or assertiveness in not being able to ask the question.

Now that you have completed this chapter you should have a good understanding of what is needed on your part to prepare for the interview. Take the time to add the material outlined in this chapter to your to-do-list.

CHAPTER 4

INTERVIEW QUESTIONS: BEHAVIORAL BASED

What are Competencies?

In selecting a person for the job, employers want to ensure that that they have certain attributes and skills. They use the term competency to be specific in what they are referring to in that particular skill. Competencies will be job specific, however, there are many that will be common to most jobs for example communication competency is almost always going to be assessed.

Examples of competencies:

- *Communication*
- *Thinking (analytical) Skills*
- *Initiative*
- *Dependability*
- *Leadership*
- *Interpersonal Awareness*
- *Teamwork*
- *Technical Expertise*
- *Entrepreneurial orientation*
- *Fostering Innovation*

This list could go on and on and it will be quite specific to the job you are seeking. You can see why it will be very important to do your research to determine which competency you need to prepare for.

In this book I cover a number of the competencies that will assist you in preparing for your interview. If the specific competency is not listed you will still get an idea of how to respond and prepare.

Benefits of understanding Behavioral Based Questions.

1. Behavioural based questions are answered based on what has happened in the past. Although this seems easy enough many people still will try and respond with answers of what they would do in a situation. This is not what the interviewer is looking for. Understanding how to answer the question bodes well with the interviewer if they do not have to try and explain the concept.

2. You will impress the interviewer if you are well prepared with your answers and if they are not using behavioral based questions, you will still have good answers to draw upon for other types of questions.

3. In preparing for behavioural based questions ahead of an interview you will see any gaps in your skills or abilities that should be attended to well before the interview.

How do you prepare for a Behavioural Based Interview?

1. Determine the Competencies

The first thing you must do is to determine the type of competencies that will be tested. You start by doing the research of the particular job that you are interested in. Talk with others that are in the position and to determine the important aspects of the job. Call the company's human resources personnel or management and ask them about the job specifications. In some cases you will get fortunate if you do a search on the internet as some job descriptions have been posted and you may find one that is relevant and lists the competencies.

The competencies most common to positions will include communication, initiative, dependability, team building, personal interaction (people skills), leadership (if applicable), flexibility, loyalty, thinking skills and ability to save or make money (if relevant). Once you have done your homework you should be able to narrow down the list that will be applicable to your interview.

2. Create your Stories

The next task is to start to create your stories. I use the word story to refer to the answer you are going to provide to answer the behavioral based question asked. By thinking of your answer in the form of a story it is much easier to prepare and remember the answer. Using the STAR method (see below) start charting down one or two good situations that will illustrate your ability in the competency. In point form identify all the items that you will want to include.

One of the best ways to answer the questions is using a format known as STAR. It is an acronym for Situation, Task, Action and Result. By structuring your answer in this way you are creating a story that is following a logical pattern from a beginning to an end.

For each of the questions in this book I have provided you with a STAR and below that what areas you may want to include. Realizing that there are so many variables to the answers you may want to include other ideas into your response.

3. Prepare a Matrix

Once you have written down all the situations that apply, it is useful if you create a chart or matrix where each of the stories is applicable. Your matrix should have all the competencies listed down one column as well as across the top of the sheet. If a situation, or story that you will be using is both a good example of dependability and initiate, indicate this in the matrix. This will assist in having a collection that can be used if the question is posed at the interview.

4. Identify any Gaps

When you are preparing your chart or matrix that will identify each of the stories, this is a good opportunity to identify where any gaps exist. Go through all the competencies and prepare your stories. Any sections that cannot be completed with a minimum of two situations can be considered a gap. This will give you a heads up that you either have to go back through your work experience to remember one, perhaps speak to your supervisor as they may have a suggestion or set out to create a situation that you will be able to use as an example. Compete this early on in the process so that you have time to prepare. The best situation is to have at least two good situations that you can draw upon to respond to the question.

CHAPTER 5

GOOD JOB INTERVIEW: THINGS TO KNOW

Do's and Don'ts

Do

1. Dress in a professional manner. Depending on your situation this may mean appearing in sharp business attire or smart casual. Look your best.

2. Arrive at the interview ahead of time so that you are sure that you have found the correct room and that you are feeling calm at your interview time

3. Be natural and show a positive attitude throughout the interview. It is important to sell yourself but ensure that you are sincere and not bragging.

4. Be calm and if you are aware of any nervous habits try and control them.

5. Listen carefully. Understand the question and if you are not sure ask for the question to be repeated.

6. Share what appeals to you about the position you are applying for and the company.

7. Look directly at the interviewer to make eye contact.

8. Briefly share your experiences, skills and background.

9. Leave when the interview is over and thank the interviewer for the opportunity. It never hurts to thank the receptionist or the person that is assisting you.

Do Not

1. Ensure that you are not wearing any strong perfume or aftershave. Any type of odor including smoking odor should not be noticeable.

2. Never argue with the interviewer.

3. Do not speak too loud or too soft.

4. Never criticize your previous employer or job. I suggest that you do not criticize anyone during the interview, stay positive

5. Never sit in any kind of defensive posture such as arms across your chest or teeter back on the chair you are in.

6. Do not discuss controversial subjects including politics and religion.

CHAPTER 6

SAMPLE JOB INTERVIEW QUESTIONS: KNOWLEDGE AND SKILL

Question

Tell me about yourself?

Purpose

General questions of this nature are used to put you at ease and to learn a little bit about you and why they should hire you. They want to learn about your background, skill level, and experience ability to get along with others and to assess your communication skills.

Sample response

"In my work experience, I have a good background in _____ (list field). This includes _____) list some of the important aspects of the job including any items that stand out). I am a very hardworking, dedicated employee that always show initiative and I feel that I am a good team member and I always get along with others. During my spare time I do volunteer work and I enjoy _____ (list a hobby). "

Question

What are your greatest strengths?

Purpose

The reason for this question is to determine the reasons for hiring you, what makes you stand out and whether you believe in yourself and are committed to the position.

Suggestions

Mention your works skills, training acquired and experience that you would offer and any job related qualities such as initiative, dependability, flexibility, reliability, enthusiasm. If you have time provide some examples of how you showed this.

Sample response

My strengths are in setting up computer networks, analyzing problems and then implementing any solutions to problems identified. I always will work independently but when required I will seek my manager's advice and guidance. I am very knowledgeable in my area of work, have always been dependable, a great team player, always assisting others, and do not mind working long hours until a job is done and go the extra mile for my employer.

CHAPTER 7

SAMPLE JOB INTERVIEW QUESTIONS: BEHAVIOURAL BASED

The samples listed below are for behavioral based questions, however, they can also be used to prepare for situational based questions. Again the only difference would be the Behavioral based questions are based on past experience where the situational based questions are open to a response as to how you would respond in a situation.

Communication

Purpose

Oral communication is often assessed during an interview by the way that the questions are answered. Typically there is no specific question asked but the interviewer will want to be able to assess your ability. Most companies will want to ensure that you are able to speak and comprehend at the level they expect for the job you are applying for.

Assessment

1. Use appropriate vocabulary and grammar
2. Answer the question in a logical, clear and concise manner.
3. Use tact and diplomacy and provide feedback if necessary
4. Use eye contact and nonverbal communication
5. Listen carefully and clarify if you do not understand any of the questions.

Things to Avoid

1. Appearing unfocused or confused
2. Acting intimidated by any of the questions
3. Using unprofessional language or slang
4. Avoid interrupting or arguing

Thinking Skills

Purpose

The purpose for assessing this skill is to determine if you have the ability to problem solve, resolve issues, analyze and identify trends. Another purpose is to see if you can take data or information given to you and come up with logical conclusions and if you would be able to determine a strategy to fix or rectify a problem. Basically do you have the skill to put your thinking, often common sense into action?

Question 1 (Thinking skills)

Describe a situation where you were faced with a difficult situation or challenging situation and how you went about solving it.

Answer Format

(**S**ituation)	Provide a real life situation.
(**T**ask)	Outline the challenging situation.
(**A**ction)	What action did you take?
(**R**esult)	What was the outcome?

Items to include

1. Provide a logical approach to the situation showing how you analyzed the problem
2. Break the scenario down in to problem areas and show a solution to various areas
3. Show common sense in the answer and be creative in solution
4. Find real cause of the problem before taking action
5. Get expert help if needed
6. Assess situation and determine the best course of action
7. Assess any impact on others and have strategies to deal with any poor outcome that affected people
8. Provide good recommendations to solving the issue

Areas to avoid

1. Not dealing with the problem
2. Not handling in timely manner
3. Only partially addressing problem leaving unresolved issues
4. Not coming up with a good response to show you have this ability

Question 2 (Thinking skills)

Describe a time when you were really resourceful in gathering information to solve a problem?

Answer Format

    (**S**ituation)   What was the problem?

    (**T**ask)   What steps did you use to gather information?

    (**A**ction)   How did you decide the information was sufficient or appropriate?

    (**R**esult)   How was the problem solved?

Items to include

1. Show you are using a logical approach to the gathering the information for the problem
2. Break the problem into smaller parts
3. Be creative
4. Draw sound conclusions for the information gathered
5. Show how you made the decision on information gathered.
6. Assess any impact.
7. Explore options if possible
8. Produce defendable decision and plan of action.

Areas to avoid

1. Not showing ability to collecting information.

2. Discussing unnecessary or unrelated information.

3. Over analyzing the problem.

4. Not solving the problem.

People Skills

Purpose

The reason for assessing this competencies is determine how you work with others including respecting others, team up and how you handle difficult situation with respect to people. These may include the skill of perceiving the needs and feelings of others, or adapting to a variety of situations where individuals and groups are involved or showing that you are able to effectively work as part of a team. There are many different questions that the interviewer may ask you but to give you a feel for the potential questions I have listed three below.

Example 1 (People Skills):

The purpose behind this question is to determine if you are able to deal with people in a respectful and sensitive manner.

Sample Question:

Tell us about a time when you were able to help a co-worker through a difficult situation?

Answer Format:

(**S**ituation)	What was it that led to the situation?
(**T**ask)	How did you become involved?
(**A**ction)	How did you help?
(**R**esult)	What was the reaction by the co-worker to your assistance?

Items to include

1. Show how you perceived the needs of another person who was experiencing a difficult time.
2. Awareness of a problem or issue that another person is facing
3. Show how you used discretion such as not gossiping about the situation to others
4. Show that you were not judgemental
5. Include any appreciation shown by the co-worker
6. Remain positive and helpful

Areas to avoid

1. Any indication that you were not sympathetic and dictated a remedy
2. Not showing understanding to the situation
3. Showing little empathy for your co-worker

Example 2 (People Skills):

This question is getting at accurately perceiving the needs and feelings of others, working well and effectively with others,

Sample Question

Describe a time when you worked effectively as part of a team?

Answer Format

(**S**ituation)   When did this happen?

(**T**ask)   What was your role?

(**A**ction)   How did you contribute?

(**R**esult)   What was the outcome?

Areas to include

1. Show you encouraged participation by others on the team
2. Discuss the various views of team members, do not make it "just about you"
3. Show you supported group decisions
4. Show that the team made group decisions

5. Did you learn or acquire new skill as a result of the team, if so tell about it

6. Were you able to use persuasion to convince others

7. Were there different needs of the team members that you had to deal with

Areas to avoid

1. Finding no positive way to deal with team members

2. Not being able to accomplish the goal set out

3. Do not come across as having to dictate solutions to team members

4. Not getting along on the team

Example 3 (People Skills):

This questions is about being able to understand the interests and concerns of others.

Sample Question

Describe a time you had a serious disagreement with your supervisor over some part of the job?

Answer Format

(**S**ituation)   What led to the disagreement?

(**T**ask)   Describe what took place?

(**A**ction)   How did you and your supervisor discuss?

(**R**esult)   What was the outcome?

Areas to include

1. Actively show how you tried to understand the position of your supervisor and others.
2. Show how you worked together to resolve the issue and compromises were made if necessary.

3. Understand the needs and feelings of others and that others have different needs, viewpoints and concerns. Show how this was respected.

4. Tried to draw out as much as you could the issue to fully understand.

Areas to avoid

1. Criticizing your supervisor.
2. Showing an unwillingness to understand and cooperate.
3. Not dealing with the conflict.
4. Not discussing the varying points of view of both you and your supervisor.

Initiative

Purpose

This competency is to show you have the ability to proactively work or contribute to achieving a goal or solving a problem.

Sample Question (Initiative):

Provide a situation where you went beyond the normal practices and go the extra mile to solve a problem or made a difference in the outcome of a situation.

Answer Format

(**S**ituation)   Describe the situation, what did you do that went beyond your normal responsibilities?

(**T**ask)   What options did you consider?

(**A**ction)   What actions did you take? Why did you select your course of action?

(**R**esult)   What was the outcome?

Items to Include

1.   How you seized an opportunity.

2. How you went up and beyond what normally would be expected.

3. How you planned and adjusted your work to accomplish the task, and that you had a full understanding of what was required to solve the problem.

4. Show how you used sound judgement, logical decision making and where necessary broke large project into smaller pieces to resolve and move forward on.

5. How you originated developed and carried through with you goal.

6. Established a set of priorities so that you were able to go the extra mile but did not leave other tasks in limbo.

7. Show how you used sound judgement, were optimistic, enthusiastic and had high energy.

Areas to Avoid

1. Willingness to accept status quo.

2. Not showing that you did go the extra mile.

3. Lack of commitment or enthusiasm.

People Management

Purpose

This particular competency focuses on the ability to plan and organize the actions and work activities of yourself and of your staff. It includes skills including developing project plans, monitoring the performance of others, setting and achieving goals and coordinating tasks. In essence it is the ability to set expectations, evaluate the effectiveness of the outputs and hold people accountable for their performance. This ability that is being assessed will be dependent on the level of job that you are being tested for. The range can be from a front end supervisor showing that you have the skill to delegate with clear direction and develop projects to a much higher level where you are tested on the ability to effectively manage and address any performance issues that arise.

Example

This example is testing your ability to show that you can set out objectives and keep activities and a project on track using resources available to you including people and money. How well do you monitor progress, the quality of work and achieve the intended goal.

Sample Question:

Describe a situation where you were responsible for a complex project?

Answer Format

(**S**ituation)   What was the project and how was it complex?

(**T**ask)   Who else was involved? What options did you consider?

(**A**ction)   What steps did you take to manage it?

(**R**esult)   Was there any employee issues? Did you manage it successfully?

Items to include

1. Set out the project in a systematic clear and objective manner
2. Set out what the priorities were
3. What became essential and not essential and how you met critical tasks
4. What staff were involved and how did you take into consideration their schedules and priorities
5. Deadlines that were met

6. Any staff issues were recognized and handled so not to create stress on staff

7. How you allowed for contingencies for unforeseen events

8. How you gathered resources to complete the project

Areas to avoid

1. Any indication that you did not clearly plan out the project

2. You do not want to give any indication that the project did not meet clear set out goals

3. Any suggestion that you were over budget or that it was not taken into consideration

CHAPTER 8

CONCLUSION

In conclusion, I hope that I have succeeded in helping you to understand what is necessary in preparing for a job interview. You will have noticed that I included a number of sample questions under the various competencies, but I must emphasize that there are any number skills and knowledge components that an employer can assess on. That will be part of your research to determine what these are. From there you can use my examples as guides to prepare your responses. I have provided you with information to do this, however, the internet is a good source of information if you feel the competency you are preparing for is not covered in the book

Do not forget to download the to-do-list checklist as a guide to start your planning. This will need to be expanded upon to include your specific material. I truly wish you success in your next interview and that your hard work pays off in getting your perfect job. Good luck.

www.ingramcontent.com/pod-product-compliance
Lightning Source LLC
Chambersburg PA
CBHW051248170526
45165CB00004B/1619